What is Kumon?

Kumon is the world's largest supplemental education provider and a leader in producing outstanding results. After-school programs in math and reading at Kumon Centers around the globe have been helping children succeed for 50 years.

Kumon Workbooks represent just a fraction of our complete curriculum of preschool-to-college-level material assigned at Kumon Centers under the supervision of trained Kumon Instructors.

The Kumon Method enables each child to progress successfully by practicing material until concepts are mastered and advancing in small, manageable increments. Instructors carefully assign materials and pace advancement according to the strengths and needs of each individual student.

Students usually attend a Kumon Center twice a week and practice at home the other five days. Assignments take about twenty minutes.

Kumon helps students of all ages and abilities master the basics, improve concentration and study habits, and build confidence.

How did Kumon begin?

IT ALL BEGAN IN JAPAN 50 YEARS AGO when a parent and teacher named Toru Kumon found a way to help his son Takeshi do better in school. At the prompting of his wife, he created a series of short assignments that his son could complete successfully in less than 20 minutes a day and that would ultimately make high school math easy. Because each was just a bit more challenging than the last, Takeshi was able to master the skills and gain the confidence to keep advancing.

This unique self-learning method was so successful that Toru's son was able to do calculus by the time he was in the sixth grade. Understanding the value of good reading comprehension, Mr. Kumon then developed a reading program employing the same method. His programs are the basis and inspiration of those offered at Kumon Centers today under the expert guidance of professional Kumon Instructors.

Mr. Toru Kumon
Founder of Kumon

What can Kumon do for my child?

Kumon is geared to children of all ages and skill levels. Whether you want to give your child a leg up in his or her schooling, build a strong foundation for future studies or address a possible learning problem, Kumon provides an effective program for developing key learning skills given the strengths and needs of each individual child.

What makes Kumon so different?

Kumon uses neither a classroom model nor a tutoring approach. It's designed to facilitate self-acquisition of the skills and study habits needed to improve academic performance. This empowers children to succeed on their own, giving them a sense of accomplishment that fosters further achievement. Whether for remedial work or enrichment, a child advances according to individual ability and initiative to reach his or her full potential. Kumon is not only effective, but also surprisingly affordable.

What is the role of the Kumon Instructor?

Kumon Instructors regard themselves more as mentors or coaches than teachers in the traditional sense. Their principal role is to provide the direction, support and encouragement that will guide the student to performing at 100% of his or her potential. Along with their rigorous training in the Kumon Method, all Kumon Instructors share a passion for education and an earnest desire to help children succeed.

KUMON FOSTERS:

- A mastery of the basics of reading and math
- Improved concentration and study habits
- Increased self-discipline and self-confidence
- A proficiency in material at every level
- Performance to each student's full potential
- A sense of accomplishment

▶▶ GETTING STARTED IS EASY. Just call us at 877.586.6671 or visit kumon.com to request our free brochure and find a Kumon Center near you. We'll direct you to an Instructor who will be happy to speak with you about how Kumon can address your child's particular needs and arrange a free placement test. There are more than 1,700 Kumon Centers in the U.S. and Canada, and students may enroll at any time throughout the year, even summer. Contact us today.

FIND OUT MORE ABOUT KUMON MATH & READING CENTERS.
Receive a free copy of our parent guide, *Every Child an Achiever,* by visiting
kumon.com/go.survey or calling 877.586.6671

Boat

To parents
Have your child trace a path through the maze with his or her finger before using a pencil. Next, have your child use a pencil to complete the maze. When your child is done, give him or her plenty of praise.

■ Draw a line through the maze from the arrow (➡) to the star (★).

1

■ Draw a line through the maze from the arrow (→) to the star (★).

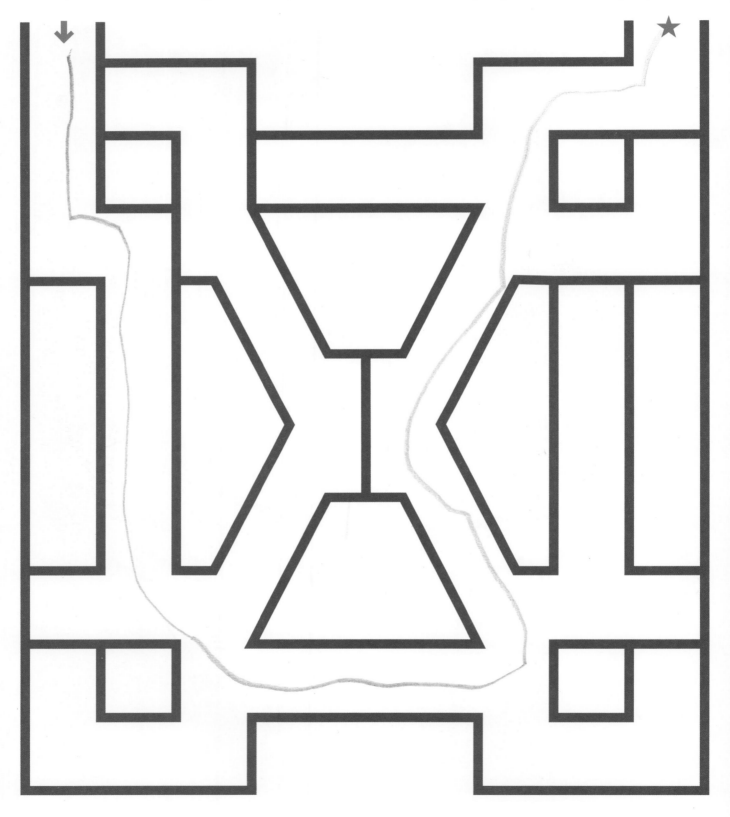

2

Name

Date

■ Draw a line through the maze from the arrow (➡) to the star (★).

3

■ Draw a line through the maze from the arrow (→) to the star (★).

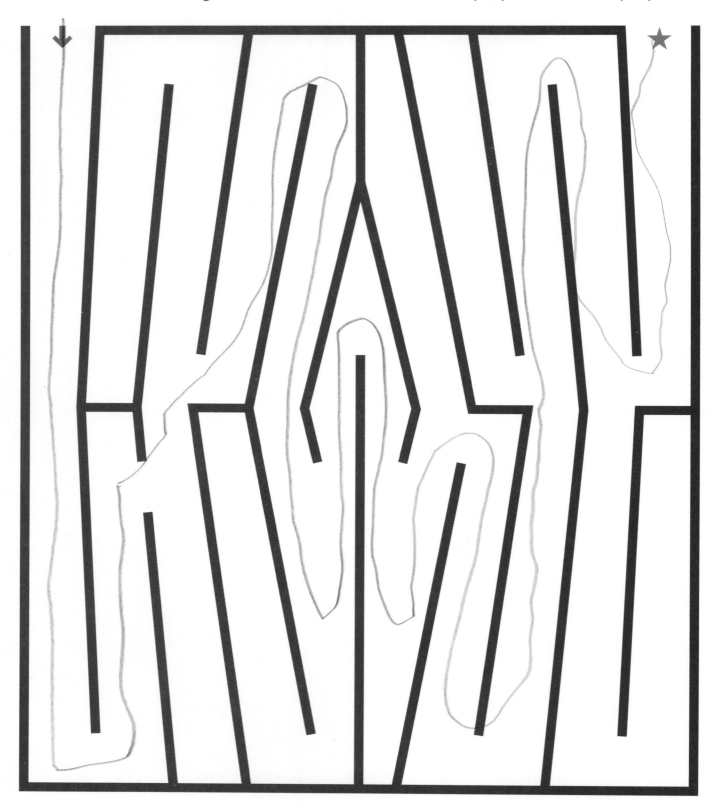

3 Submarine

Name

Date

■ Draw a line through the maze from the arrow (→) to the star (★).

5

■ Draw a line through the maze from the arrow (→) to the star (★).

6

Cargo Plane

Name

Date

■ Draw a line through the maze from the arrow (➜) to the star (★).

7

■ Draw a line through the maze from the arrow (➡) to the star (★).

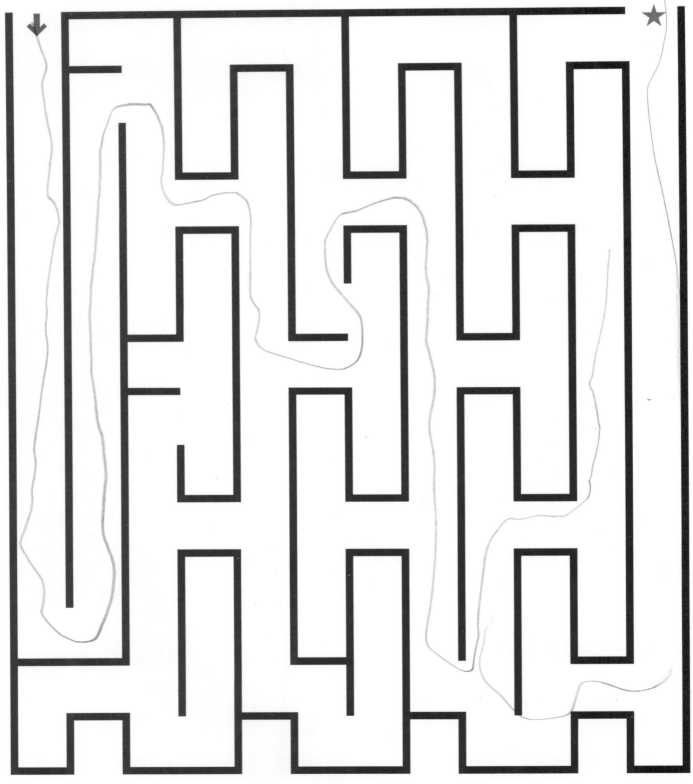

5 Motorcycle

Name

Date

■ Draw a line through the maze from the arrow (➡) to the star (★).

9

■ Draw a line through the maze from the arrow (➡) to the star (★).

6 Classic Car

Name

Date

■ Draw a line through the maze from the arrow (➡) to the star (★).

■ Draw a line through the maze from the arrow (→) to the star (★).

Name

Date

■ Draw a line through the maze from the arrow (➡) to the star (★).

13

■ Draw a line through the maze from the arrow (➡) to the star (★).

Name

Date

■ Draw a line through the maze from the arrow (➡) to the star (★).

■ Draw a line through the maze from the arrow (➡) to the star (★).

9 Motor Scooter

Name

Date

■ Draw a line through the maze from the arrow (➡) to the star (★).

17

■ Draw a line through the maze from the arrow (➡) to the star (★).

10 Racing Bike

■ Draw a line through the maze from the arrow (➡) to the star (★).

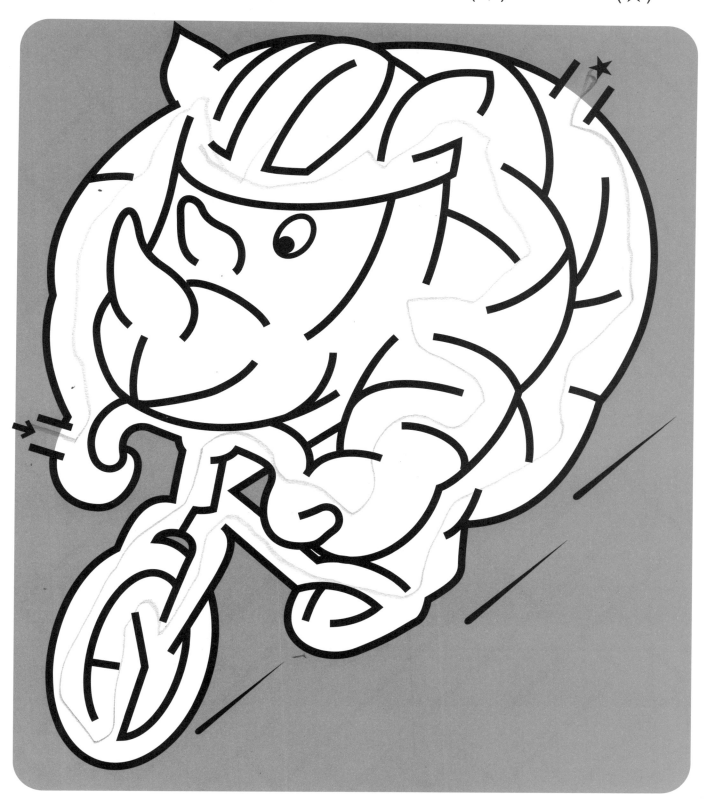

■ Draw a line through the maze from the arrow (➡) to the star (★).

Big Motorcycle

Name

Date

■ Draw a line through the maze from the arrow (➡) to the star (★).

21

■ Draw a line through the maze from the arrow (➡) to the star (★).

Name	
Date	

■ Draw a line through the maze from the arrow (➡) to the star (★).

23

■ Draw a line through the maze from the arrow (➡) to the star (★).

 **Convertible**

■ Draw a line through the maze from the arrow (➔) to the star (★).

25

■ Draw a line through the maze from the arrow (➡) to the star (★).

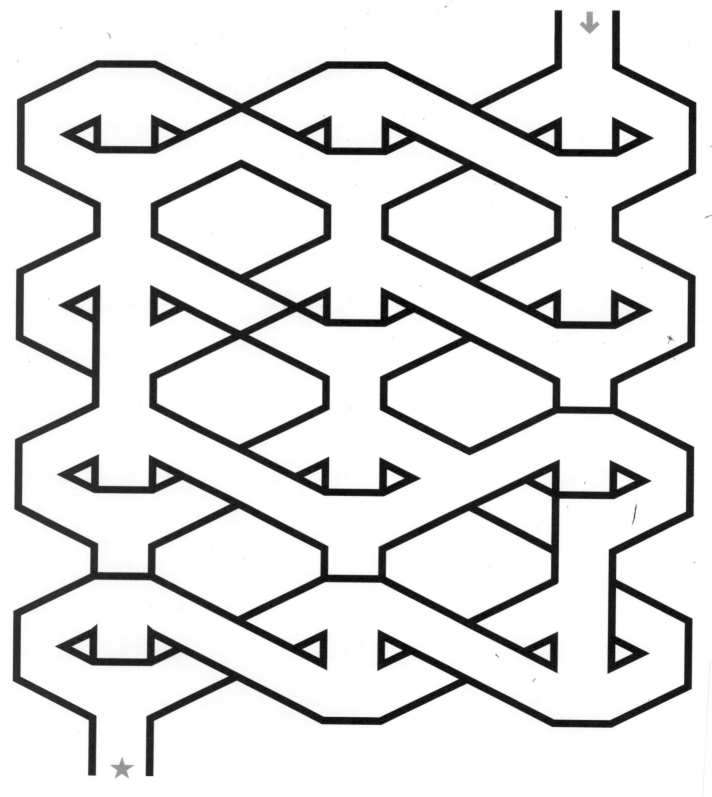

26

Name

Date

■ Draw a line through the maze from the arrow (➡) to the star (★).

■ Draw a line through the maze from the arrow (➡) to the star (★).

28

15 Bulldozer

Name

Date

■ Draw a line through the maze from the arrow (➡) to the star (★).

■ Draw a line through the maze from the arrow (➡) to the star (★).

30

Name

Date

■ Draw a line through the maze from the arrow (➜) to the star (★).

■ Draw a line through the maze from the arrow (➡) to the star (★).

32

Stunt Airplane

Name

Date

To parents
If your child has difficulty, try giving him or her a hint.

■ Draw a line through the maze from the arrow (➔) to the star (★).

33

■ Draw a line through the maze from the arrow (↑) to the star (★).

34

Big Propeller Plane

Name

Date

■ Draw a line through the maze from the arrow (➜) to the star (★).

■ Draw a line through the maze from the arrow (↑) to the star (★).

19 Small Propeller Airplane

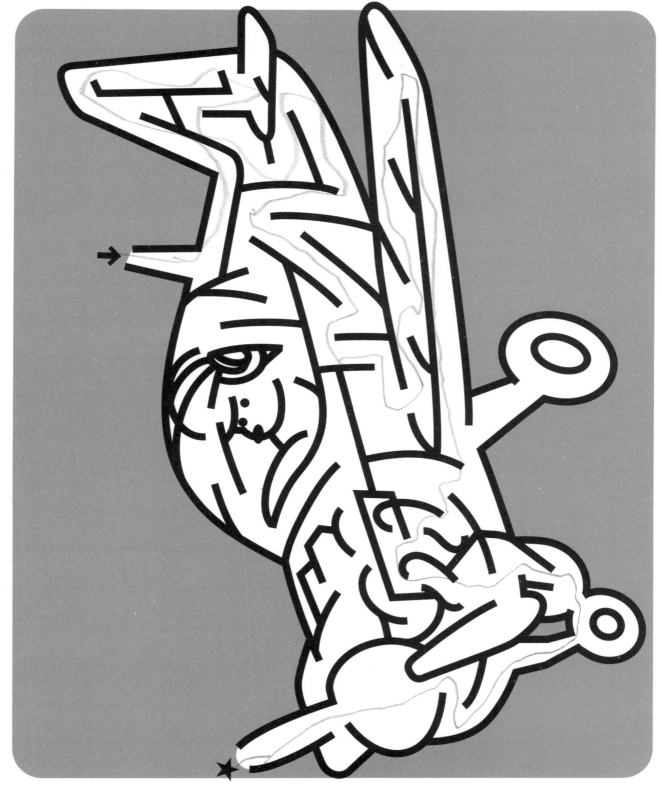

Draw a line through the maze from the arrow (→) to the star (★).

■ Draw a line through the maze from the arrow (↑) to the star (★).

38

Helicopter

Name

Date

Draw a line through the maze from the arrow (↑) to the star (★).

■ Draw a line through the maze from the arrow (↑) to the star (★).

Go-Cart

Draw a line through the maze from the arrow (➔) to the star (★).

41

Draw a line through the maze from the arrow (↑) to the star (★).

22 Cement Mixer

Draw a line through the maze from the arrow (➔) to the star (★).

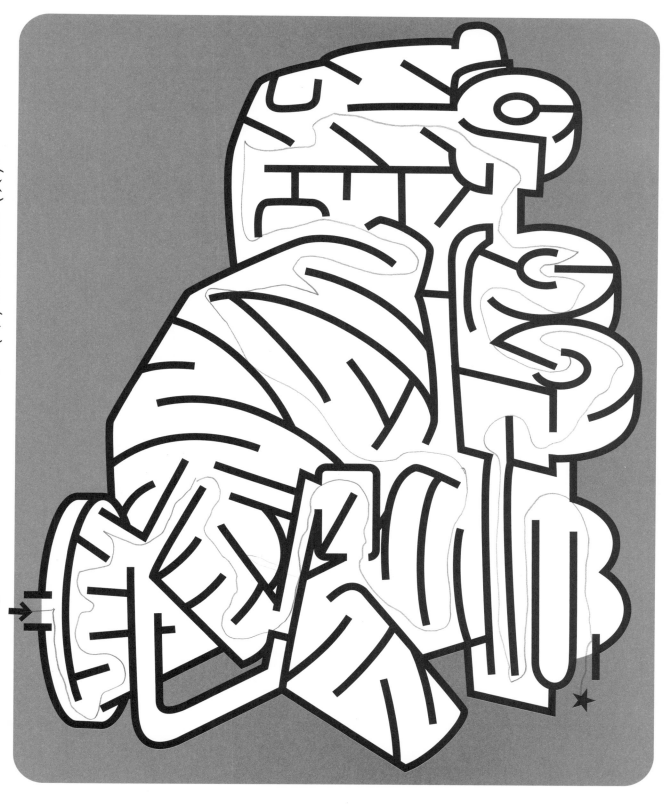

43

■ Draw a line through the maze from the arrow (➡) to the star (★).

23 Hydrofoil Boat

Name

Date

■ Draw a line through the maze from the arrow (→) to the star (★).

45

■ Draw a line through the maze from the arrow (↑) to the star (★).

46

Cargo Ship

Name

Date

Draw a line through the maze from the arrow (➔) to the star (★).

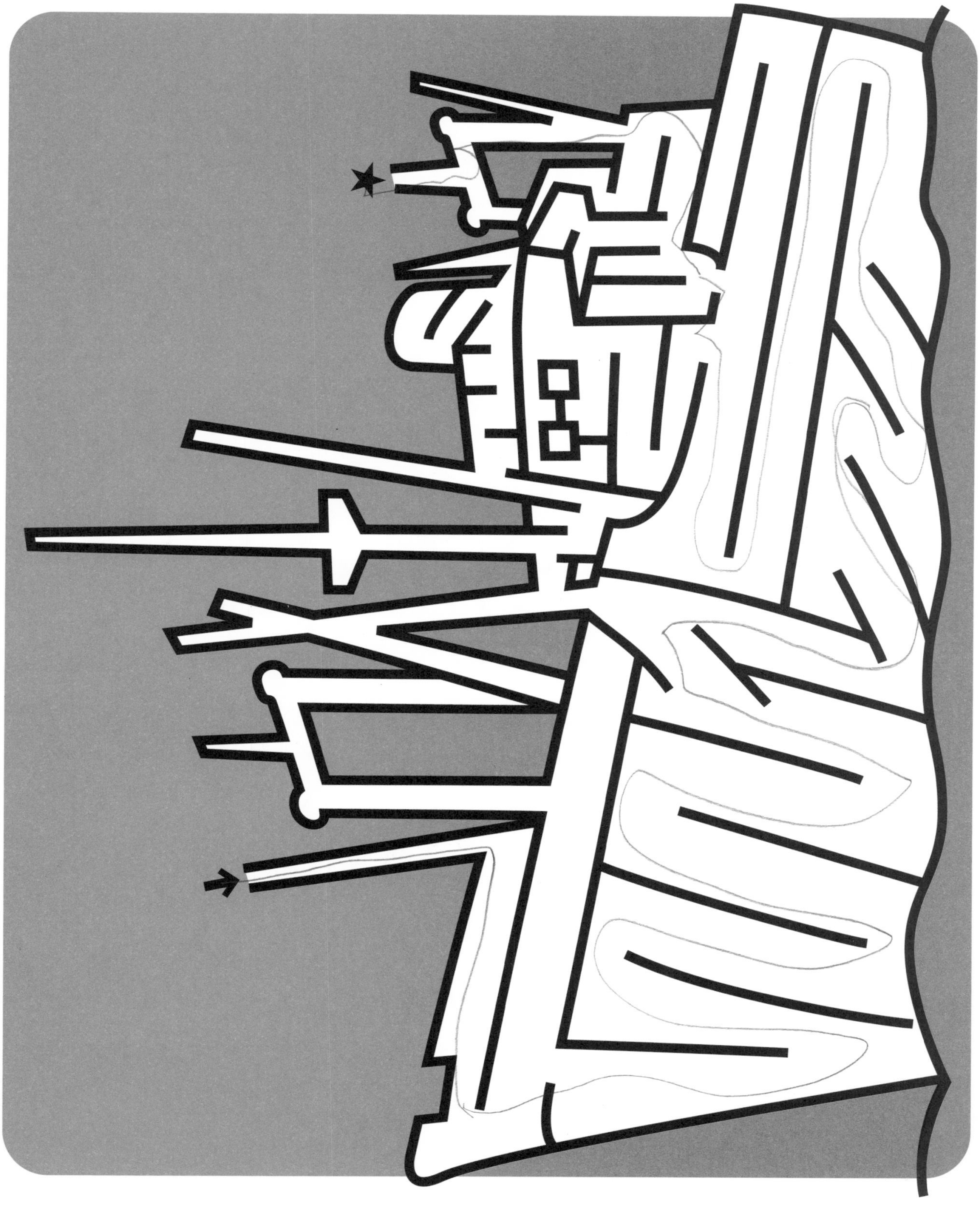

47

■ Draw a line through the maze from the arrow (↑) to the star (★).

25 | **Hovercraft**

■ Draw a line through the maze from the arrow (➔) to the star (★).

49

Draw a line through the maze from the arrow (↑) to the star (★).

50

Transport Plane

Name

Date

Draw a line through the maze from the arrow (➔) to the star (★).

51

■ Draw a line through the maze from the arrow (↑) to the star (★).

27 Biplane

Draw a line through the maze from the arrow (➔) to the star (★).

■ Draw a line through the maze from the arrow (↑) to the star (★).

54

Sailing Ship

Draw a line through the maze from the arrow (➔) to the star (★).

Draw a line through the maze from the arrow (↑) to the star (★).

56

29 **Cruise Ship**

Name

Date

■ Draw a line through the maze from the arrow (➜) to the star (★).

57

■ Draw a line through the maze from the arrow (↑) to the star (★).

58

Fireboat

Name

Date

Draw a line through the maze from the arrow (→) to the star (★).

■ Draw a line through the maze from the arrow (↑) to the star (★).

60

31 Electric Train

■ Draw a line through the maze from the arrow (➔) to the star (★).

■ Draw a line through the maze from the arrow (↑) to the star (★).

Steamroller

Draw a line through the maze from the arrow (➜) to the star (★).

■ Draw a line through the maze from the arrow (↑) to the star (★).

33 Classic Car

Name

Date

Draw a line through the maze from the arrow (→) to the star (★).

65

■ Draw a line through the maze from the arrow (↑) to the star (★).

Dump Truck

Name

Date

Draw a line through the maze from the arrow (➜) to the star (★).

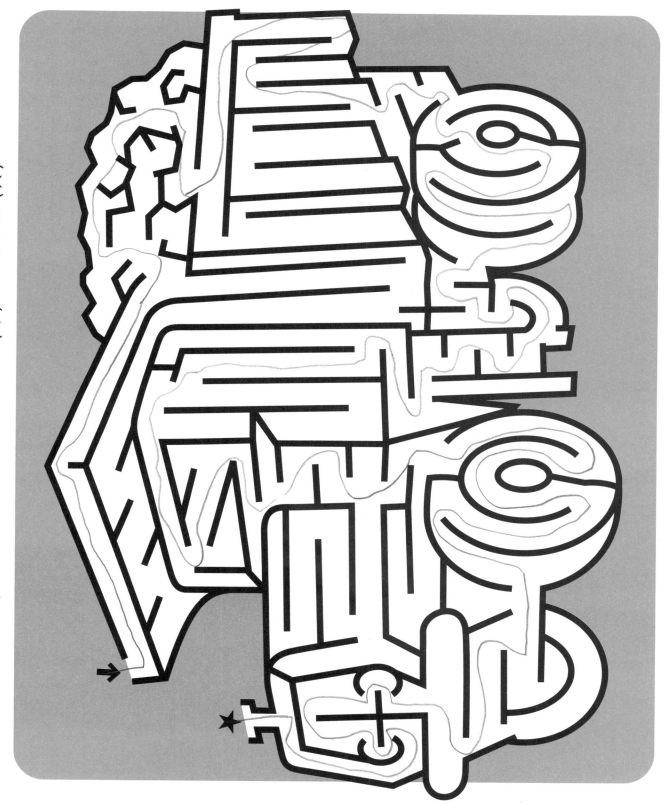

■ Draw a line through the maze from the arrow (↑) to the star (★).

Big Rig

Draw a line through the maze from the arrow (➔) to the star (★).

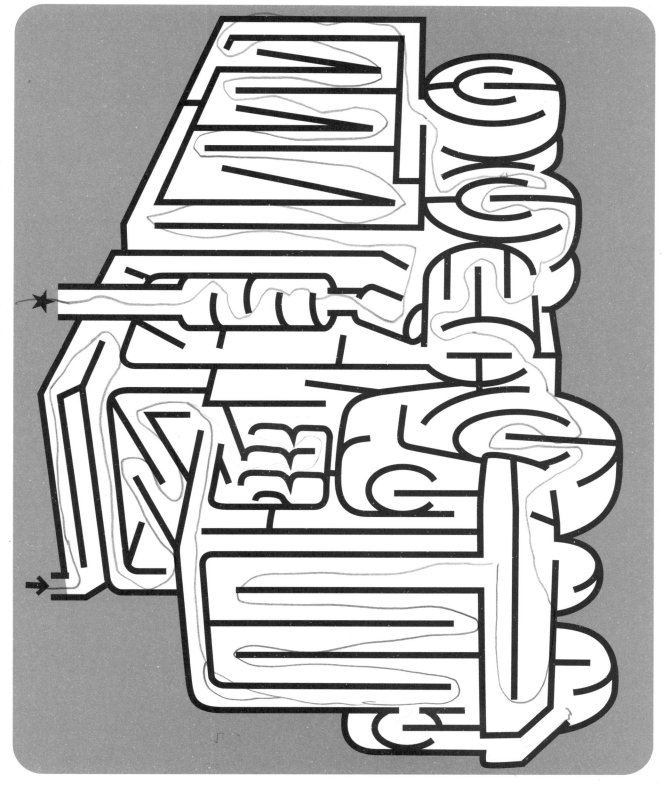

■ Draw a line through the maze from the arrow (↑) to the star (★).

70

Backhoe

Draw a line through the maze from the arrow (➔) to the star (★).

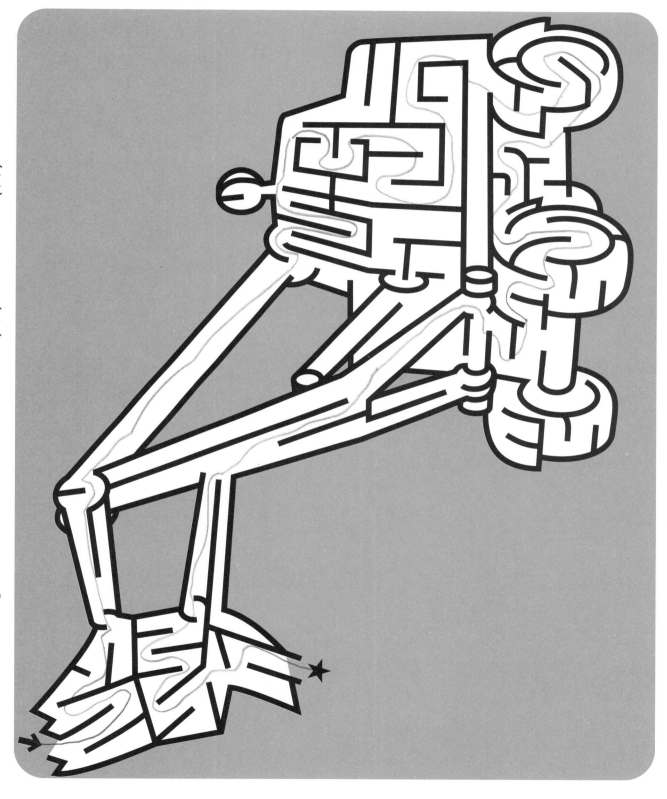

■ Draw a line through the maze from the arrow (↑) to the star (★).

37 | Steam Train

Name

Date

Draw a line through the maze from the arrow (➜) to the star (★).

73

■ Draw a line through the maze from the arrow (↑) to the star (★).

74

Fire Engine

Draw a line through the maze from the arrow (↑) to the star (★).

■ Draw a line through the maze from the arrow (➜) to the star (★).

76

Space Shuttle

Draw a line through the maze from the arrow (→) to the star (★).

Draw a line through the maze from the arrow (⬆) to the star (★).

78

40 Space Station

Name

Date

Draw a line through the maze from the arrow (➔) to the star (★).

79

To parents
Did your child enjoy these mazes? When your child is finished, compare this page with the first few pages of this workbook. You will see considerable progress in his or her ability to control a pencil. Please give praise for your child's effort and achievement.

■ Draw a line through the maze from the arrow (↑) to the star (★).

KUM◯N

Certificate of Achievement

Lindsay Li

is hereby congratulated on completing

My Book of Mazes: Things That Go!

Presented on _____Feb 10_____ , 20_15_

Yufeng Wen

Parent or Guardian